Field Events

in Action

Bobbie Kalman

🌱 Crabtree Publishing Company

www.crabtreebooks.com

Created by Bobbie Kalman

Dedicated by Hadley Dyer
For Adam, my big little brother

Editor-in-Chief
Bobbie Kalman

Writing team
Bobbie Kalman
Hadley Dyer

Substantive editor
Kathryn Smithyman

Project editor
Kristina Lundblad

Editors
Molly Aloian
Kelley MacAulay

Art director
Robert MacGregor

Design
Margaret Amy Reiach

Production coordinator
Katherine Kantor

Photo research
Crystal Foxton

Consultant
Pat Mooney, Head Cross-Country and Track and Field Coach,
  Clarion University of Pennsylvania

Special thanks to
Josh Fenton, Eric Emery, Kyle Emery, Michael Emery,
and Cambridge Track and Field Club

Photographs
Marc Crabtree: pages 10 (right), 11 (top and middle), 16 (left),
  26 (bottom)
Icon SMI: Philippe Millereau/DPPI: page 4; Glyn Kirk/Action
  Plus: page 5; STL: page 22; Frank Faugere/DPPI: page 24
Jeff Jacobsen/KUAC: page 28
© PHOTOSPORT.COM: back cover, title page, pages 10 (left),
  11 (bottom), 12, 14, 15, 16 (right), 17, 18, 19, 27 (top), 31 (right)
Duane Hart/sportingimages.com.au: pages 23, 25, 27 (bottom), 29
Other images by Corel, Digital Stock, Image 100 and Photodisc

Illustrations
All illustrations by Bonna Rouse except:
Katherine Kantor: page 13

Crabtree Publishing Company

www.crabtreebooks.com   1-800-387-7650

Cataloging-in-Publication Data
Kalman, Bobbie.
  Field events in action / Bobbie Kalman.
    p. cm. -- (Sports in action)
  Includes index.
  ISBN 0-7787-0340-1 (RLB) -- ISBN 0-7787-0360-6 (pbk.)
  1. Track and field--Juvenile literature. I. Title. II. Series.
  GV1060.55.K35 2004
  796.42--dc22

                                    2004014182
                                    LC

**Published in
the United States**
PMB16A
350 Fifth Ave.
Suite 3308
New York, NY
10118

**Published
in Canada**
616 Welland Ave.,
St. Catharines, Ontario,
Canada
L2M 5V6

**Published in the
United Kingdom**
73 Lime Walk
Headington
Oxford
OX3 7AD
United Kingdom

**Published
in Australia**
386 Mt. Alexander Rd.,
Ascot Vale (Melbourne)
VIC 3032

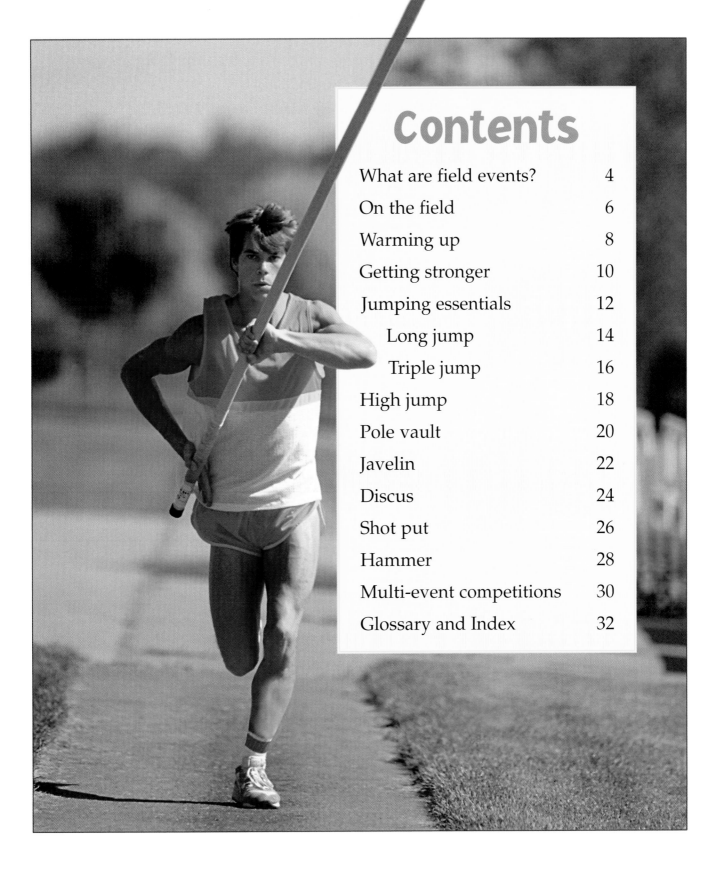

Contents

What are field events?

Field events are contests that test the throwing and jumping abilities of athletes. In throwing events, athletes compete to throw objects the farthest. In jumping events, athletes compete to jump the longest distances or the greatest heights. Field events are part of a group of sports called track and field. **Track events** are running and walking races. Athletes compete in track-and-field events at competitions known as **track-and-field meets**.

Throwing and jumping

Most field competitions consist of four jumping events and four throwing events. The jumping events are **long jump**, **triple jump**, **high jump**, and **pole vault**. Each throwing event is named after the object that the athlete throws: **javelin**, **discus**, **shot put**, and **hammer**. Keep reading to find out more about each field event.

Throwing equipment

The javelin is a lightweight spear that is pointed on one end.

Discus: The discus looks like two dinner plates stuck together. It is 8.25 inches (21 cm) in **diameter**. It is made of wood or plastic and has a metal rim.

Shot put: The shot used in shot put is a heavy, solid ball made of metal such as iron or brass.

Hammer: The hammer is a metal ball attached to a metal wire, which has a handle at the other end. The ball is similar to the one used in shot put.

Ancient Olympics

Track-and-field meets have a long history. The ancient Greeks created several field events almost 3,000 years ago. Throwing and jumping events were part of the original Olympic Games held in the city of Olympia, Greece. Only men competed in the ancient Olympics. A Roman emperor stopped the Olympic Games about 1,000 years after they began.

Modern Olympics

In 1896, the Olympics started up again in Athens, Greece. The Olympics included many track-and-field events. They were for men only until 1928, when women's events became part of the Olympics. Pole vault and hammer throw for women were not included until the year 2000 at the Olympics in Sydney, Austrailia.

Carl Lewis has won a total of four Olympic gold medals in long jump. He is shown above performing at the 1996 Olympic Games in Atlanta, Georgia.

On the field

Track-and-field events take place inside a **stadium**. During a track-and-field meet, track athletes compete on the **track**, shown below. At the same time, field competitions take place on a grassy area within the track or on fields near the track. Field athletes must not allow themselves to be distracted by the track events going on around them. Each field event has its own area with plenty of space for athletes to run, jump, and throw safely. During competitions, **meet officials**, or judges at track-and-field meets, are also on the field. They make sure the athletes perform according to the rules of each event. In most field events, athletes get three **attempts**, or tries, to throw or jump. The athletes with the best performances move on to the next round.

The field

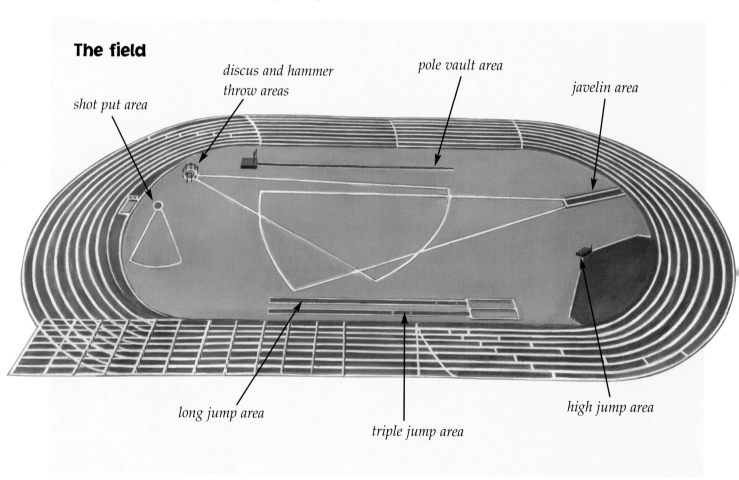

shot put area

discus and hammer throw areas

pole vault area

javelin area

long jump area

triple jump area

high jump area

What to wear?

When you practice or compete in field events, it is best to wear clothing that is designed for movement and comfort.

A young athlete might wear a pair of shorts and a sleeveless shirt called a **singlet**. During meets, field athletes are identified by numbers. A different number is pinned to each competitor's singlet.

A field uniform usually consists of a singlet and shorts. Both boys and girls can choose the length of their shorts. Some girls wear shorts that are similar to swimsuit bottoms.

Field footwear

Proper shoes are essential to an athlete. Choose shoes that hug your feet tightly but are still comfortable for running. Running or **cross-training** shoes cushion your feet and ankles as they hit the ground while you run and jump. Experienced athletes wear special shoes for competitions. Some wear shoes with spikes on the bottom. The spikes are near the front of the shoes. They help athletes' feet grip the ground so they will not slip when they are jumping or throwing.

spike

Warming up

Field events require you to use different muscles in your body. Your muscles must be **flexible** and strong. To gain flexible, strong muscles, you must warm up and stretch your muscles before and after each practice or meet. Warming up also helps prevent injuries. Walk or jog for about five minutes to loosen up your muscles and get your heart pumping. Be sure to stretch your muscles slowly. Move into each position carefully and only stretch as far as you can without feeling pain. The stretches will become easier as you become more flexible. While warming up, many athletes wear long pants and long-sleeved shirts to keep their muscles warm.

Quadriceps stretch

Stand on your right foot and lift your left foot behind you until you can grab your ankle with your left hand. Pull gently on your left ankle until you feel a stretch along the front of your left thigh. Hold for fifteen seconds. Repeat with the right leg.

Hamstring stretch

Sit on the floor with your right leg straight in front of you. Bend your left leg and place your foot along the inside of your right knee. Bend forward slightly until you feel a stretch up the back of your right leg. Hold for fifteen seconds. Repeat with your left leg forward.

Ankle rotations

Sit with your left leg extended in front of you. Bend your right leg until the lower part of your leg is resting across your left thigh. Grab your foot and gently turn it around in circles. When you have done ten circles, do ten more in the other direction. Remember to change legs!

Hip flexor stretch

Stand with your feet shoulder-width apart. Step out as far as you can with your right leg. Lower your left knee to the floor and place the top of your foot on the floor. Move your hips forward until your right knee is directly over your toes. Place your hands on your right thigh for support. Hold for fifteen seconds and then switch legs.

Neck stretches

Stand with your legs shoulder-width apart and hold your arms by your sides. Slowly turn your head and look over your left shoulder, keeping the rest of your body still. Hold the stretch for ten seconds. Return your head to the starting position, then turn it to the right. Hold the stretch on that side and then return to the starting position. Slowly lower your head to your chest. Hold this position for ten seconds. Slowly, tilt your head back until you are looking up at the ceiling and hold the stretch.

Getting stronger

Once you have warmed up, you can move on to the **training drills** shown on this page. Training drills help you practice the specific skills you need for each event. The drills will help you run quickly and keep your body fit.

Being fit is important in all events. Next, try the strength-training exercises shown on the next page to build your muscles and keep them strong. Being strong will help you jump and throw farther.

Sprints

Sprints are short, fast runs that train your body to move with maximum energy. To practice sprints, run 100 feet (30.5 m) as fast as you can and then walk until you catch your breath. Then perform the sprint again. At first, you will likely get tired quickly and your sprints will slow down. With more training, you will be able to sprint farther without losing speed.

Jumping rope

To train your heart, lungs, and muscles to work harder, you need to lift your legs. Jumping rope is a great exercise for your legs. Jump rope in place for three minutes. Then jump rope while slowly jogging forward for 100 feet (30.5 m). Finally, jump rope while jogging backward for 50 feet (15.2 m).

Push-ups

To perform a push-up, lie face-down on the ground, with your hands on the floor beneath your shoulders. Straighten your arms to push yourself up, holding your body rigid from head to toe. Your body should be in a straight line, and your weight should be resting on your hands and your toes. Lower yourself down until your nose is about four inches (10 cm) from the floor. Repeat ten times.

Crunches

To perform a crunch, lie on your back and put your hands behind your head. Bend your knees and place your feet flat on the ground. Press your lower back against the floor and slowly lift your shoulders off the floor. Lower yourself back down. Repeat ten times.

A helping hand

Jumping events involve high jumps and powerful landings, which can result in injuries if they are not done correctly. Throwing incorrectly during throwing events can also lead to injuries. A field athlete should always be supervised by a **coach**. A coach will teach you how to perform the moves required of each field event. He or she will correct your mistakes and offer you advice. A coach can also help you set goals that will strengthen your body and improve your skills over time.

Jumping essentials

Each field event is a different sport. Athletes who perform in one event have different skills than the athletes who perform in other events. The jumping events involve similar skills and techniques, however. In each event, an athlete runs along a **runway**, or running path, performs a **takeoff** to jump into the air, and then lands in a **landing pit**.

Jumping terms

Athletes use several terms to talk about jumping events. Some common terms are listed below.

Run-up: a fast run along a runway during which an athlete gains the speed and power needed for a jump; also called an **approach**

Takeoff: the point at which an athlete leaves the ground to perform a jump or a **vault**

Takeoff board: a flat piece of wood positioned at the end of the runway, which helps a long jump or triple jump athlete in his or her takeoff

Crossbar: a **horizontal** bar that is held up by two **upright bars**, over which a pole vaulter or a high jumper must jump

Landing: the position of an athlete's body at the end of a jump or a vault

Runways

Each jumping event has a specially designed runway and a landing pit. The runways for long jump, triple jump, and pole vault are all straight and long to give athletes plenty of room for their run-ups. The high jump runway is fan-shaped to allow high jumpers to jump over the crossbar from either the right side or the left side.

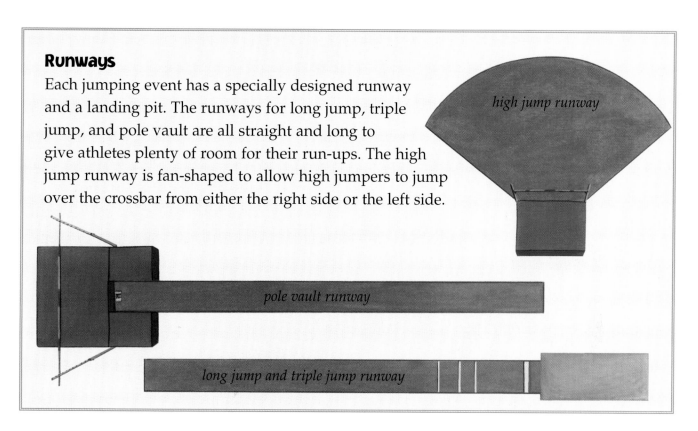

high jump runway

pole vault runway

long jump and triple jump runway

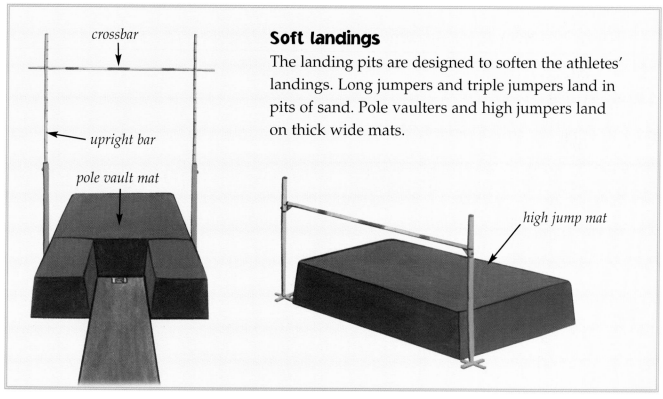

crossbar

upright bar

pole vault mat

Soft landings

The landing pits are designed to soften the athletes' landings. Long jumpers and triple jumpers land in pits of sand. Pole vaulters and high jumpers land on thick wide mats.

high jump mat

Long jump

In long jump, athletes compete to jump the farthest distances. An athlete begins by running quickly down the runway. At the takeoff board, the athlete leaps into the air and lands feet first in the sand pit. The length of the jump is measured from the takeoff board to the first mark that the athlete's body makes in the sand.

The two most common jumping techniques are the **hang** technique and the **hitch kick**. These terms describe the way an athlete's body moves as it travels through the air. Young athletes usually start with the hang technique because the hitch kick is more difficult to perform. The hitch kick often results in farther distances, however.

Hanging around

When your foot hits the takeoff board, begin your jump by **running off the board**, or driving the knee of your lead leg into the air. Your **lead leg** is the leg that you lift first. The other leg, which is called the **takeoff leg**, pushes your body off the ground before joining the lead leg in the air. While in the air, pull both legs back so your knees are slightly behind your body. It will seem as if you are "hanging" in the air for a few seconds. You can improve your jump by using your arms. As you jump, swing your arms backward and then circle them up and over your head to help move you forward. To lengthen your jump, push your feet forward as you land.

The hitch kick

To perform the hitch-kick technique, extend your lead leg during your takeoff. Once you are in the air, swing your lead leg backward and your takeoff leg forward so that your legs pass each other as they change positions in the air. Bring your lead leg forward again so that both feet are together for the landing.

Long jump training

To train for long jump, practice both sprinting and leaping. A fast sprint is an important part of your run-up. The number of steps in your run-up often matches your age. For example, a thirteen-year-old athlete will take about thirteen steps before he or she jumps. It takes practice to discover the number of steps that works best for you. As you practice, you'll learn how to time your run-up so you perform your takeoff with your preferred foot.

When your feet hit the sand, it's best to rock forward. If you fall backward, your distance will be shorter.

Triple jump

As in long jump, triple jump athletes compete to jump the farthest distances. After performing a run-up, a triple jump athlete must perform three moves—a hop, a step, and a jump—between the takeoff and the landing. The triple jump involves a difficult combination of moves and requires excellent coordination and timing. The main challenge for the triple jumper is to maintain enough speed and power for all three moves. In a competition, a triple jump is measured from the takeoff mark to the first mark the athlete's body makes in the sand.

Hop to it!

A good triple jump begins with a powerful hop. To hop, take off from, and land on, the same leg. Use your strongest leg for the hop. To find out which leg is the strongest, see how far you can hop forward on each leg. First hop three times on one leg. Then hop forward three times on the other leg. Which leg carried you farther? Use the leg that carried you the farthest for the hop.

Run-up

Perform the run-up as fast as you can. A fast run-up will lead to a more powerful hop. Your run-up takes you to the takeoff mark on the runway, where you start your hop. If you begin your hop from beyond the takeoff mark, you will be **disqualified**, or taken out of the competition.

Hop

When you hop, you do not need to hop very high. Instead, focus on hopping as far forward as you can. Drive your other knee up to help push you forward. To hop farther, swing your arms forward. Pull your arms back as you land to prepare for the step.

Step

From the hop, take a big step forward onto your other leg. Swing both arms forward during the step to keep you moving forward. It takes practice to learn how to end up in the correct spot for the jump into the sand pit, but if you do not land in the pit, your jump won't count!

Jump

After you have taken the step, pull both knees up and push your feet forward for the landing. Pulling your arms back and up over your head as you jump will help you jump farther. Rock forward on the landing. If you fall backward, your distance will be shorter.

High jump

High jumpers compete to jump over a crossbar. The athlete who clears the bar at the highest height without knocking it off the upright bars wins the competition.

The run-up

Before you start your run-up, think about which leg is your lead leg. Remember, your lead leg is the one you lift first. If your right leg is your lead leg, then you should approach the bar from the right side of the runway. If your left leg is your lead leg, you should approach the bar from the left side of the runway. The distance of your run-up may be as long or as short as you need it to be. The last part of your run-up should curve in toward the bar, so that the line of your run-up creates a "J" shape.

lead leg

takeoff leg

Jumping high

You are ready to jump when you are in front of the middle section of the bar. Push off with your takeoff leg and swing your lead leg upward. The swinging motion of your lead leg turns your body so your back is to the bar as you leap backward. To carry you upward, pull up your takeoff leg until it is beside your lead leg in the air.

Soaring higher

In high jump competitions, the athletes who jump over the bar successfully go on to the next round. The bar is raised for each round. Meet officials choose the starting height and the rate at which the height of the bar increases.

High jumpers may skip their turns at a certain height and go on to compete at the next height. They may not go back down in height, however. The athlete who jumps the highest wins. When athletes tie, the competitor with fewer misses wins.

Clearing the bar

When you take off, swing your arms upward and then quickly pull them in to your sides as you go over the bar. Arch your back and push your hips upward. Once your backside is over the bar, pull your legs toward your chest. Your body is allowed to touch the bar as you move over it, but the bar cannot fall down!

Coming down

Relax your body a little once you are safely over the bar. Raise your head and shoulders slightly. You should land on your back and shoulders and then roll up toward your neck.

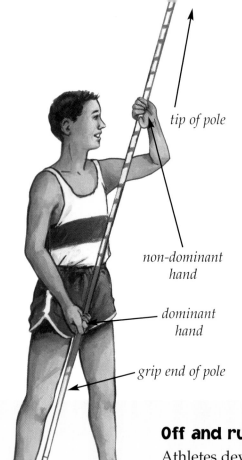

tip of pole

non-dominant hand

dominant hand

grip end of pole

Pole vault

Pole vault is an event in which a competitor uses a long pole to lift his or her body over a crossbar that is set very high. The pole is made out of a strong material that can bend many times without breaking. The bending action of the pole shoots the pole vaulter up and over the crossbar. The athlete who clears the crossbar at the greatest height is the winner. Pole vault is a challenging event. Most athletes do not begin this sport until they are teenagers.

Off and running

Athletes develop their own pole-vaulting styles. You can carry the pole on the right or the left side of your body. The length of the run-up can be as short or as long as you need it to be. A fast run-up will give you a powerful vault. At the beginning of the run-up, hold your pole in a **vertical**, or up-and-down, position, as shown top left. As you approach the takeoff area, lower the tip of your pole into the **pole vault box**, which is sunk into the ground at the end of the runway.

Pole plant

Just before your takeoff, raise the grip end of the pole so that your dominant arm is fully extended above your head. Plant the tip of the pole into the pole vault box. The pole vault box helps prevent the pole from slipping when it is planted. To raise your body into the air, push the pole forward, toward the landing pit, with your non-dominant hand. Pull downward on the grip end of the pole with your dominant hand. This move will cause the pole to bend. The bending action of the pole drives your body upward.

Up and over

Drive your lead leg upward to help lift your body. As your takeoff leg joins your lead leg in the air, raise your hips above your shoulders. Straighten out your body so it is in line with the pole. Drive your feet up over your head. Use your hips and rotate your body so that you are looking down the pole as you push yourself over the crossbar. Let go of the pole once you have pushed yourself over the crossbar.

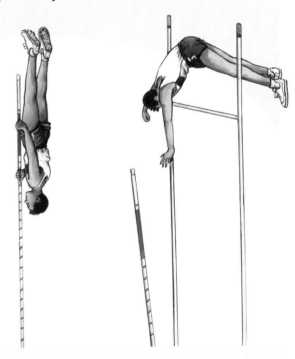

Back to earth

Your feet will go over the crossbar first, followed by your body. As you fall, prepare to land on your back. Landing on your back helps prevent injuries, such as twisting an ankle or hurting your neck.

Javelin

In ancient Greece, soldiers trained and competed to throw spears as far and as accurately as possible. Javelin is a modern version of this ancient event. Javelin is a distance contest, but good aim is still important. An athlete performs a run-up and then throws the javelin as far as possible using one hand. The distance of the throw is measured from the **foul line** to where the javelin first lands on the ground. The athlete who throws the farthest wins. Athletes must follow safety rules when they throw javelins so that nobody on the field or in the stands gets hurt. Many schools do not offer javelin as part of their track-and-field programs, so you may not have a chance to try javelin until you are older.

An athlete must grip the javelin with his or her palm facing upward, as shown above.

The run-up

Use a running start to gain speed and **momentum**, or driving power, before you throw the javelin. Carry the javelin above your shoulder, with the palm of your hand facing upward. After you have taken about five steps, pull the javelin back so your throwing arm is behind you as you run. Lean back in the final steps of your run-up. Leaning back puts your body into position to throw the javelin up into the air. The javelin is now behind your body. Perform one or more **cross-steps** to keep your feet moving forward and to allow your upper body to lean back. Aim the javelin so it lands inside the **sector**, or fan-shaped landing area.

Through the air

When you throw the javelin, push your front hip forward and then drive your chest and shoulder forward as you throw the javelin high up into the air. Your body must face forward, and the throw must come from above your shoulder. The tip of the javelin must land in the sector, but it doesn't have to stick into the ground. After you throw the javelin, make sure you do not keep running too far forward, or you will step over the foul line.

Cross-steps

The athlete above is right-handed. He cross-steps by stepping his right leg in front of his left leg when the javelin is behind his body. By cross-stepping, he is able to lean far back so he is in position to throw the javelin high into the air.

23

Discus

Discus is an event in which an athlete throws a discus as far as possible from within a **throwing circle**. The distance of the throw is measured from the edge of the throwing circle to the spot in the sector where the discus first lands. Competitors must not step outside the throwing circle until the discus has landed. The athlete who throws the farthest wins. Throwing the discus takes a strong hand and a powerful arm. An athlete throws a discus by spinning his or her body for one-and-a-half rotations. The rotations help you build momentum before you launch the discus through the air.

The sides and back of the discus throwing circle are surrounded by a wire safety net or cage that protects onlookers. The discus throw can be a dangerous event because it is easy to drop the discus or to release it unexpectedly.

Starting position

Hold the discus by curving your fingertips slightly over the edge of the discus. Start your throw by facing the back of the throwing circle. Stand with your feet shoulder-width apart. Hold the discus at arm's length in front of your body. Sweep the discus in front of your body at about chest level and then sweep it back until it is behind your shoulder, as shown on page 24. One or two practice sweeps will get you ready to throw. As you sweep, twist your body slightly and shift your weight from foot to foot.

Spin cycle

To create momentum, perform one-and-a-half quick turns within the circle. Your throwing arm will trail behind your body as you turn, creating a whiplike action when the discus is thrown. The turns increase the distance the discus flies when you release it at the front of the throwing circle. Keep your throwing arm straight.

A beginner uses a discus that weighs 2.2 pounds (1 kg), but an experienced thrower uses a heavier one.

Releasing the discus with your arm high in the air (shown right) helps the discus travel farther. The discus should spin as it flies through the air. If it wobbles, it will not travel as far.

Shot put

The object of the shot put event is to heave the shot as far as possible. Although the shot put is called a "throwing event," athletes actually push the shot from their shoulders rather than throw it. The shot put is a test of power. Throwers use their entire bodies to push the shots as far as possible.

Shots weigh between 1.1 pounds (0.5 kg) for beginners and sixteen pounds (7.25 kg) for experienced athletes.

Inside the circle

Shot put takes place inside a throwing circle, shown below. The throwing circle is surrounded by a metal rim. There is a raised **stop-board** at the front of the circle. The athlete must not touch the top of the stop-board or any area beyond the circle.

The starting position

Start by holding the shot under your chin or alongside your neck. Hold the shot in one hand at the base of your middle three fingers. Balance the shot above the palm of your hand, with your thumb and little finger.

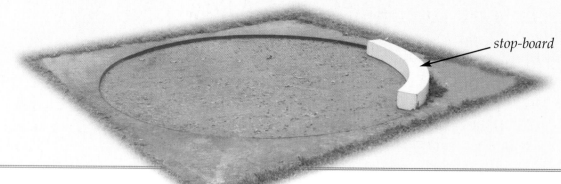

stop-board

Putting the shot

The first thing you need to learn is how to push the shot from your shoulder. Start at the back of the throwing circle, facing away from the field. As you turn your body in the direction of the throw, straighten your arm and push the shot away from your body with all your strength. Once you know how to **put**, or push, the shot properly, try the two techniques described below to help you gain momentum. Momentum will help you push the shot farther.

This athlete holds her elbow high to keep the shot in the correct position.

The glide technique

When using the **glide technique**, crouch down low and lean over the rear edge of the throwing circle. Kick one leg back, toward the front of the circle, so you **glide**, or slide, backward on the other leg. As you move, turn your body toward the front of the circle. The shot must stay in contact with your neck until the final part of the move.

The rotational technique

Once you have perfected the glide technique, you can try the **rotational**, or turning, technique. The turns in the rotational technique are similar to the turns performed by discus throwers. Spin your body one-and-a-half times to gain momentum before releasing the shot.

A put is measured from the stop-board to the place where the shot lands. It must land within the sector, or the throw won't count!

Hammer

Hammer throw is a contest of strength and balance. A hammer thrower uses the same throwing circle as a discus athlete uses. The throws are measured according to the same rules as the rules of the other throwing events. Unfortunately, many spectators miss this event because it is not safe for it to take place while track events are in progress. Young athletes do not usually compete in hammer throw until they are in high school. Hammer throw must be performed in a safe area under the supervision of a coach. The starting hammer weight is twelve pounds (5.4 kg) for boys and 8.8 pounds (4 kg) for girls.

Holding a hammer

If you are right-handed, hold the handle in your left hand. Then close your right hand over your left hand and place the ball of the hammer on the ground next to your right foot. If you are left-handed, hold the handle in your right hand, place your left hand over your right hand, and place the ball of the hammer next to your left foot. You can practice by using a ball inside a sack or net.

Round and round

To throw a hammer, stand at the back of the throwing circle and face the opposite direction from which you will throw. Without twisting your body, swing the hammer around your head a couple of times to gain momentum. The hammer should be at different heights as it **rotates**, or turns around. For example, when the hammer is in front of your body, it should be close to the ground, and when it is behind your body, it should be higher. Hammer throw athletes call these swings "the winds."

Heave ho!

After swinging the hammer two or three times, your entire body will begin to rotate along with the hammer. Hold the hammer in front of your body and spin your whole body around in three or four tight circles. Beginners usually turn only once or twice. As you turn, move toward the front of the throwing circle. With each turn, you gain speed. Finally, when you reach the front of the circle, release the hammer backward over your shoulder. You are not allowed to leave the throwing circle until the hammer has landed on the ground.

As your body rotates, bend your knees but keep your upper body straight.

Multi-event competitions

Multi-event competitions are popular with athletes who excel at more than one track-and-field event. In these competitions, each athlete competes in several events. Men compete in the **decathlon**, which is made up of ten events. Women compete in the **heptathlon**, which includes seven events. The **pentathlon** is a five-event competition in which both men and women compete.

In the pentathlon, athletes of different ages compete in different events. In multi-event competitions, points are awarded to athletes for the distances, heights, or times they receive in each event. An athlete does not need to win every event, but he or she should have the ability to do well in all the events combined. Multi-event athletes spend years training before they are able to win competitions.

The decathlon

The decathlon is a test of both strength and speed. The competition takes place over two days, during which the athletes compete in long jump, high jump, pole vault, shot put, javelin, and discus. Decathlon athletes must also compete in four track events. The track events are 100 **meter** (m), 400m, and 1500m races, as well as 110m **hurdles**, shown below. Points are awarded to the athletes based on their performances in each event. When all the competitions are over, the points are added up to determine the winner.

The heptathlon

The heptathlon is a two-day, seven-event competition. Women compete in the following track events: 200m, 800m, and 100m hurdles. They also compete in shot put, javelin, long jump, and high jump events. Heptathlon athletes must be in excellent shape to master all seven events.

Glossary

Note: Boldfaced words that are defined in the book may not appear in the glossary.

cross-training Describing training in different sports, such as running, walking, and bicycling

diameter The length of a straight line passing through the center of a circle

flexible Capable of being bent easily into various positions

foul line A mark on the ground over which an athlete's body is not allowed to cross

horizontal Describing something that is parallel to the ground

hurdles A track event in which athletes must leap over small fences called hurdles as they run

meter A measurement equaling 3.3 feet or about one yard

pole vault box A box sunk into the end of the pole vault runway into which the pole is placed to prevent it from slipping

sector The area in which a throwing-event object must land for the throw to count

stadium A large building that holds a playing field for a sporting event and seats from which people can watch

throwing circle The area from which an athlete throws an object

training drill An exercise that is repeated in order to teach and perfect a skill or procedure

upright bar One of two bars holding up the crossbar in pole vault or high jump

vault To jump or leap over an object or barrier, especially with the help of a pole

Index